INSTANT SPANISH

INSTANT
SPANISH

by Dorothy and David Thomas

Editorial Consultant:
Diego Aguirre de Carcer

Illustrated by DRAGONFLY DESIGNS

dot publications

New edition 1991
Copyright © DM & DWS Thomas 1988, 1990

Published by dot Publications
54A Haig Avenue, Whitley Bay NE25 8JD, U.K.

ISBN 1 871086 04 3

Printed by Charter Press Ltd., Rhuddlan, North Wales

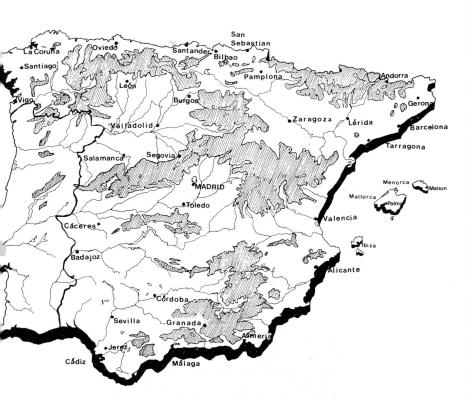

Contents

Introduction

If you've never spoken a word of a foreign language before, or you've forgotten everything you learned at school, your problems are now over.

With dot Publications' *Instant* phrasebooks you can find what you need fast. Just follow the speech guides beneath each picture.

First we help you pronounce it right with the easy guide on page 7. As well as the pronunciation, we show you where to put the emphasis by setting the right word or part of a word in **heavy** type.

Next we take you through a series of typical tourist situations, giving you the words you'll need to get what you want, followed by some idea of the replies you are likely to hear.

In most cases we give you a basic situation which can be used in lots of places – for example, the phrases used in the baker's shop dialogue on page 24 can be used to buy things in most other kinds of shop as well.

If you want to go a little further with the language, at the back you'll find a short section explaining the most important points of Spanish grammar.

Right at the back, on page 80, is a list of numbers. Learn these first if you can – numbers are a vital part of any language and will make shopping, booking things and just talking to people very much easier.

Remember, travel abroad should be fun, and making your way in the local language is a big part of it. We hope to help you enjoy yourself on your trip.

¡Buen viaje!

Spanish Sounds

We have tried to keep our transcription as simple as possible, so that you can read the questions and answers almost as if they were English. Some syllables are in **heavy** type to show you where the stress comes. Some words are also split by a hyphen to make them easier to read and to get the stress in the right place: pronounce them as one word, with no gaps.

a short, as in "mat": *casa* (house)
ay like "eye": *playa* (beach)
b and *v* sound roughly the same, a very soft "b": *vino* (wine)
*c** as in "call": *cama* (bed)
but before *e* and *i* like "th" in "thick": *cinco* (five)
d as in English, but between vowels and at the end of a word like the soft "th" in "mother": *usted* (you)
e often like "e" in "met": *cuenta* (bill)
sometimes like "a" in "date": *queso* (cheese)
g as in "go", except before *g* and *i* when it resembles the guttural "ch" of "loch": *Gerona* (We have often used "h" to represent this sound)
h is silent: *hombre* (man)
i like "ee" in "meet",
but before another vowel like "i" in "view": *tiempo* (time)
j "ch" in "loch" (like guttural *g*): *jamón* (ham)
*ll** like "lli" in "million" or "y" in "yes": *calle* (street)
*ñ** like "ni" in "onion": *mañana* (tomorrow)
o short, as in "not": *ocho* (eight)
qu like "k" in "key": *¿qué?* (what?)
rr strongly rolled: *perro* (dog)
s as in "test" (never "z"): *adiós* (goodbye)
u as in "book": *mucho* (much); silent after *q* and in the combinations *gue* or *gui*: *guitarra* (guitar). After other consonants often like "w" in "twenty".
v same as *b*
x between vowels like English "x"; before consonants more like "s": *expreso* (express)
y alone or at the end of a word, like "ee" in "meet",
otherwise as in "yes": *yo* (I)
z like "th" in "thick": *zumo* (juice)

* in the dictionary, **ch** comes at the end of the **c's**; similarly **ll** and **ñ** are found at the end of their sections.

In Latin America and Southern Spain *c* before *e* and *i*, and *z* are pronounced "s". *ll* is often like "y" in "yes".

Stress Rules. If a Spanish word ends in a vowel, *n* or *s*, stress the last syllable but one (*ia* counts as one syllable). If a word ends in any consonant except *n* or *s*, the last syllable is stressed. Exceptions are marked by an accent ´.

HOTELS

Spain has lots of hotels, graded from 1-5 stars. You can stay in an international Hotel **H** or state-run *Parador* (often a historic building or castle), or in a more modest *Hostal* **Hs** or *Pensión* **P**. A *Fonda* **F** is an unpretentious inn, of similar standard to a *Casa de huéspedes* **CH** or boarding house. If you want a private room look for *Habitaciones* or simply *Camas,* which means beds. N.B. A *Residencia* does not serve meals. If you have a complaint ask for the *libro de reclamaciones,* a legal requirement for all hotels.

If you've booked

1. Hola, buenas tardes.

3. Tengo una habitación reservada a nombre de Jones.

2. Buenas tardes.

4. De acuerdo. Es la habitación diez. Su pasaporte, por favor. Y ¿Me firma aquí?

RECEPCIÓN

1. *Ola, **bway**nass **tar**dess.*
   Good evening.

3. ***Tengo** oona abby-tath**yon** ray-**cair**vath*a *a **nom**bray day Jones.*
   I have booked a room in the name of Jones.

2. ***Bway**nass **tar**dess.*
   Good evening.

4. *Day ak**wair**do. Ess la abby-tath**yon** dee-**eth**. Soo passa**por**tay, por fav**vor**. Ee may **feer**ma a-key?*
   Of course. It's room 10.
   May I have your passport and could you sign here, please?

If you *haven't* booked, and you find this sign on the door, or if the receptionist says: "Está completo" *(Es-**sta** kom**play**to)*, it's full. If you *have* booked, go on in anyway. If not, try another hotel and turn the page.

habitación y desayuno
room with breakfast

media pensión
half-board

pensión completa
full-board

In most towns the Tourist Information Office will fix a hotel booking for you (many speak English). Look for *Oficina de Turismo* or this sign:

una noche	dos noches
oona nochay	*doss nochess*
one night	two nights

1. Buenas tardes. ¿Tienen una habitación para esta noche?
2. Sí, tenemos. ¿Para cuántas personas?
3. Para dos personas (y dos niños).
4. Muy bien. ¿Para cuántas noches?
5. Para una noche.

1. *Bwaynass tardess. Tyaynen oona abby-tathyon parra esta nochay?*
   Good evening. Have you a room for tonight?

2. *See, tenaymoss. Parra kwantass pairsonass?*
   Yes, for how many people?

3. *Parra doss pairsonass (ee doss neenyoss).*
   For two people (and two children).

4. *Mwee bee-en. Parra kwantass nochess?*
   Fine. For how many nights?

5. *Parra oona nochay.*
   For one night.

	doble	
	dobblay	
	double	
	individual	
	indeevid-wal	
	single	
	el baño	
	el banyo	
	the bath	
	la ducha	
	la doocha	
	the shower	
	los servicios	
	loss sairvith-yoss	
	the lavatory	

1. ¿Qué prefiere, una habitación doble o individual?
2. Una doble y dos individuales.
3. ¿Con baño o sin baño?
4. Con baño.

1. *Kay prayfee-ayray, oona abby-tathyon dobblay o indeevid-wal?*
   Would you like a double room or a single?

2. *Oona dobblay ee doss indeevid-wal-ess.*
   A double and two singles.

3. *Kon banyo o seen banyo?*
   With bath or without?

4. *Kon banyo.*
   With bath.

1. *See, te**nay**moss oona abby-tath**yon** **lee**bray. Ess la abby-tath**yon** dee-**eth**y-ocho.*
   Yes, we have a room available, it's number 18.

3. *Sonn kwattro meel pess**ay**tass por **noch**ay.*
   It's 4000 pesetas a night.

★
¿Dónde se puede aparcar?

***Don**day say **pway**thay appar-**kar**?*
Where can I park?

2. *Mwee bee-**en**. Kay **preth**yo **tyay**nay?*
   Good. How much is it?

4. *Day ak**wair**do, la kee-**ay**ro.*
   Fine. I'll take it.

1. *Bee-**en**. Komo say **lya**mma oo**steth**?*
   Good. What is your name, please?

2. *May **lya**mmo Baker.*
   My name is Baker.

3. *May **day**-ha soo passa**por**tay, por fav**vor**?*
   Could I have your passport, please?

4. ***Grath**yass. A-key **tyay**nay soo **lya**vvay.*
   Thank you. Here is your key.

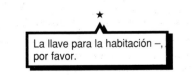

★
La llave para la habitación –, por favor.

*La **lya**vvay parra la abby-tath**yon** –, por fav**vor**.*
   May I have the key to room –, please.

Inspecting the room

1. ¿Puedo ver la habitación?

2. Si, ¿cómo no?

3. *(If you like it)* Muy bien, la quiero.

— OR —

(If you don't)
No, no me gusta. Es demasiado ruidosa (pequeña). ¿No tiene algo mejor?

4. Lo siento, señor …

1. **Pway**tho vair la abby-tath**yon**?
   May I see the room?

2. *See, komo no?*
   Yes, of course.

3. *Mwee bee-**en**, la kee-**ay**ro.*
   Good, I'll take it.

4. *Lo siento, señor …*
   I'm sorry sir …

— OR —

*No, no may **goo**sta. Ess demmass**yath**o rweet**hos**a (pekk**ayn**-ya). No **tyay**nay algo may-**hor**?*

No, I don't like it. It's too noisy (small). Have you anything better?

Meals at the hotel

2. De ocho y media a diez.

1. ¿A qué hora es el desayuno? (la comida/el almuerzo – la cena)

Checking out

1. ¿Puede darme la cuenta, por favor?

2. Adiós.

1. *A kay ora ess el dessa-**yoo**no? (la kom**mee**tha – la **thay**na)*
   What time do you serve breakfast? (lunch-dinner)

2. *Day ocho ee **may**th-ya a dee-**eth**.*
   From 8.30 to 10.

1. **Pway**thay **dar**may la kwenta, por fav**vor**?
   Please may I have the bill?

2. *Add-**yoss**.*
   Goodbye.

(Time p.71)

(Methods of payment p.33)

RENTED ACCOMMODATION

Finding your Apartment

You will generally know the name of your landlord or landlady, so just ask:

Por favor, ¿dónde vive la señora – (el señor –)?

*Por fav**vor**, **don**day **vee**vay la sen**yor**a – (el sen**yor** –)?*
Excuse me, where does Mrs. – (Mr. –) live?

AT THE VILLA
The kitchen – La cocina – *La Ko**thee**na*

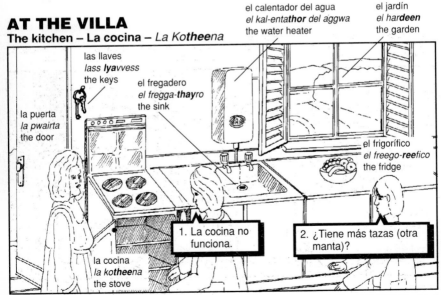

el calentador del agua
*el kal-enta**thor** del **ag**gwa*
the water heater

el jardín
*el har**deen***
the garden

las llaves
*lass **lya**vvess*
the keys

el fregadero
*el fregga-**thay**ro*
the sink

la puerta
*la **pwair**ta*
the door

el frigorífico
*el freego-**ree**fico*
the fridge

1. La cocina no funciona.

2. ¿Tiene más tazas (otra manta)?

la cocina
*la ko**thee**na*
the stove

1. *La ko**thee**na no foonth-**yo**na.*
   The stove isn't working.

2. ***Tyay**nay mass **tath**ass? (otra manta).*
   Have you any more cups (another blanket)?

12

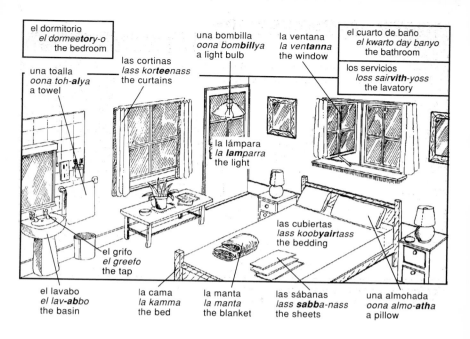

el dormitorio
el dormeetory-o
the bedroom

una bombilla
oona bombillya
a light bulb

la ventana
la ventanna
the window

el cuarto de baño
el kwarto day banyo
the bathroom

los servicios
loss sairvith-yoss
the lavatory

una toalla
oona toh-alya
a towel

las cortinas
lass korteenass
the curtains

la lámpara
la lamparra
the light

las cubiertas
lass koobyairtass
the bedding

el grifo
el greefo
the tap

el lavabo
el lav-abbo
the basin

la cama
la kamma
the bed

la manta
la manta
the blanket

las sábanas
lass sabba-nass
the sheets

una almohada
oona almo-atha
a pillow

una taza
oona tatha
a cup

un vaso
oon vasso
a glass

un plato
oon platto
a plate

una cacerola
oona kathay-rola
a saucepan

la mesa
la maysa
the table

un tenedor
oon tenaythor
a fork

basuras
bassoorass
rubbish

un paño de
cocina
*oon panyo day
kotheena*
a tea-towel

una sartén
oona sarten
a frying pan

una silla
oona seel-ya
a chair

una cafetera
oona kaffay-tayra
a coffee pot

una jarra
oona harra
a jug

un cuchillo
oon koochill-yo
a knife

una cuchara
oona koocharra
a spoon

13

Camping

*Oy-ga por fav**vor**,
eye oon **kam**ping
por a-key?*
    Excuse me, is
    there a campsite
    near here?

1. *Po**thay**moss akkam**par**
  a-key?*
    May we camp here?

3. *Parra oona/doss
  nochess* (oona
  se**manna**).*
    One/two* nights
    (a week).

2. *See. Kwanto tee-**empo**
  pee-**en**sa kay**thar**say?*
    Yes. How many
    nights do you want
    to stay?

Campsite signs

PROHIBIDO ACAMPAR	No Camping
AGUA POTABLE	Drinking water
NO MALGASTE EL AGUA	Don't waste water
SERVICIOS	Toilets
CABALLEROS	Men
SEÑORAS	Women
BASURAS	Rubbish
NO TIRAR BASURAS	No Rubbish
RESIDUOS QUIMICOS	Chemical Toilet Disposal Point
PROHIBIDO HACER FUEGO	No Fires

1. *Ee parra **kwan**tass pair**son**ass?*
  How many are there of you?

3. *Te**nay**moss oon **koch**ay ee oona
  tee-**en**da/karra**vann**a/**koch**ay
  kamma.*
    We have a car and a tent/
    caravan/motor caravan.

2. *Parra doss a-**dul**toss y
  oon/doss/tress* **neen**yoss.*
  Two adults and
  one/two/three* children.

(*See numbers on page 80)

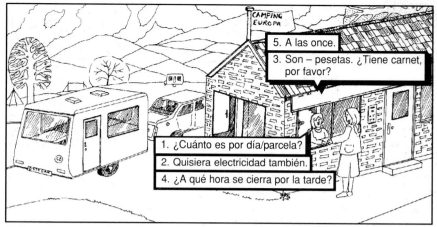

1. *Kwanto ess por **dee**-a/ parthayla?*
   How much does it cost per day/pitch?

3. *Sonn – pess**ay**tass. **Tyay**nay **kar**nay, por fav**vor**?*
   That will be – pesetas. Have you a carnet, please?

2. *Keesee-**ay**ra aylektri-thi**dath** tamb-**yen**.*
   I'd like electricity (a hook-up) too.

4. *A kay ora say thee-**ay**ra por la **tar**day?*
   What time do you close in the evening?

5. *A lass **on**thay.*
   At 11 o'clock.

International Camping Carnet

Widely accepted at campsites overseas as an identity document. Though seldom obligatory, it is useful not to have to leave your passport in reception. You'll need it for things like changing money after all.

Albergue Juvenil	Refugio
*Al**bair**gay hoovenn**eel***	*Ref**foo**hee-o*
Youth Hostel	Mountain Hut

1. ***Bway**nass tardess. **Tyay**nay **kam**mass parra esta **noch**ay?*
   Good evening. Have you any beds for tonight?

3. *A-key es-**sta** mee **kar**nay day albair-**gee**sta.*
   Here's my membership card.

2. *See, tengo.*
   Yes, I have.

4. ***Tyay**ness oon sakko day dor**meer**?*
   Have you a sleeping bag?

EATING OUT

Virtually everywhere, bar, tasca, bodega, cervecería or taberna, serves drinks. It's cheaper to drink at the bar than be served at a table or outside. Most places serve tapas (small bar snacks) too, sometimes free but usually for a small charge. There's a wide choice of tapas (***tapp**ass*).

If you want a larger portion, ask for una ración de … (*oona rath-**yon** day*/a portion of …) gambas (*gambass*/shrimps), calamares (*kal-am**mar**ess*/squid), aceitunas (*a-thay**too**nass*/olives), tortilla (*tor**teel**-ya*/Spanish omelette), jamón serrano (*ham-**on** serr**anno**/*cured ham).

Churrerías serve churros (***chew**ross*) (ask for una ración), made from doughnut-type batter and often eaten with a drink of hot chocolate. You can get a full meal at a restaurante, cafetería or mesón. Marisquerías serve fish and seafood. Una hamburguesa (*oona amboor**gay**sa)* is a hamburger.

Platos combinados are one-course meals with meat/fish and vegetables served on the same plate. Typical choices are huevos con jamón (ham and eggs), chuletas (chops) or pollo asado con patatas fritas (roast chicken and chips). There's usually a picture of each and a number. Use the number to order, e.g. El plato combinado número cuatro, por favor (*el platto kombeena-tho **noo**mayro kwattro, por fav**vor**). If you don't know the name of something, say Quisiera uno así (*Keesee-**ay**ra oono a-**see**/*I'd like one like that).

MEALS

el desayuno (*el dessa-**yoo**no*)	–	continental breakfast.
la comida/el almuerzo (*la kom**mee**tha/el alm**wair**tho*)	–	lunch, main meal of the day, served from about 2.00 p.m.
la cena (*la thayna*)	–	supper, never served before 8.30 p.m. and often later, especially in the south.

¡Salud!　　　　　　　　　　　　　　¡Qué aproveche!
*Sa-**looth**!*　　　　　　　　　　　*Kay appro-**vay**chay!*
Cheers!　　　　　　　　　　　　　　Enjoy your meal!

Ordering drinks and snacks

un bocadillo
*oon bokka**deel**-yo*
a sandwich

un vino blanco
oon veeno blanco
a white wine

una cerveza
*oona thair**vay**tha*
a beer

un zumo de piña
oon thoomo day peenya
a pineapple juice

con hielo
*kon ee-**ay**lo*
with ice

1. ¿Qué desean?
2. Quisiera un café solo, un jerez y un zumo de naranja.
3. ¿Qué bocadillos (tapas) tiene?
4. Jamón, queso y chorizo.
5. Pues, uno de jamón y dos de queso.

1. *Kay dess**ay**an?*
   What would you like?
3. *Kay bokka**deel**-yoss (**tapp**ass) **tyay**nay?*
   What sandwiches (bar snacks) have you got?
5. *Pwess, oono day ham-**on** ee doss day **kay**so.*
   One ham and two cheese, then.

2. *Keesee-**ay**ra oon kaff**ay** solo, oon herr**eth** ee oon thoomo day na-**ran**ha.*
   I'd like a black coffee, a sherry and an orange juice.
4. *Ham-**on**, **kay**so ee chorr**ee**tho.*
   Ham, cheese and sausage.

Paying, finding the lavatory

←SERVICIOS

1. ¿Dónde están los servicios?
2. La cuenta, por favor.

1. ***Don**day est-**an** loss sair-**vith**yoss?*
   Where is the lavatory?
2. *La **kwenta**, por fav**vor**.*
   The bill, please.

3. ¿Está ocupada?

3. *Es-**sta** okkoo**patha**?*
   Is this (seat/table) taken?

17

Breakfast

1. *Oy-ga, por fav**vor**!*
   Excuse me!

3. *El dessa-**yoo**no, por fav**vor**.*
   I/We'd like breakfast, please.

2. ***Bway**noss **dee**-ass. Kay van a tom**mar**?*
   Good morning. What would you like?

4. *Pod**ree**-ya **dar**may …?*
   Could I have some …?

un café (con leche) *oon kaffay (kon lechay)* a coffee (with milk)	leche ***lech**ay* some milk		pan/bollos/ tostadas *pan/**bol**yoss/ tost-**ath**as* bread/rolls/ toast
	caliente/fría *kal-**yen**tay/**free**-a* hot/cold	un chocolate *oon choko**lah**-tay* a chocolate	mantequilla/ mermelada *mantay-**keel**ya/ mairmay-**lath**a* butter/jam

Restaurants — Booking a table

1. *¿Puedo reservar una mesa para cuatro a las nueve?*

2. *¿Su nombre, por favor?*

1. ***Pway**tho raysair**var** oona maysa parra kwattro a lass noo-**evv**ay?*
   May I book a table for four at nine o'clock?

2. *Soo **nom**bray, por fav**vor**?*
   Your name, please?

See page 38 for how to cope with Spanish telephones.

1. **Tyay**nay oona maysa
   parra tress, por fav**vor**?
   Have you a table for three,
   please?

2. *Oon momento ... a raysair-vatho?*
   Just a moment ...
   Have you booked?

¿Tiene platos vegetarianos?

★

*Tyaynay **platt**oss
vayhaytarry-**ann**oss?*
   Have you any vegetarian dishes?

Ordering a meal

1. *El menú, por favor.*

2. De primero – menestra
   de verduras, y de
   segundo – bistec con
   ensalada y patatas fritas.

4. ¿Tomarán postre?

3. ¿Qué nos aconseja para
   el niño (los niños)?

5. ¿Cómo se llama esto?

1. *El men-**oo**, por fav**vor**.*
   The set menu, please.

3. *Kay noss akkon**say**-ha parra el
   neenyo (loss **neen**yoss)?*
   What do you suggest for the
   child (the children)?

5. *Komo say **Iya**mma esto?*
   What's this called?

2. *Day pree**may**ro – men**est**ra day
   vair**doo**rass, ee day seg**oon**do –
   bee**stekk** kon ensa-**lath**a ee
   patt**att**ass **free**tass.*
   First – vegetable soup, and to
   follow – steak with salad and
   chips.

4. *Tommar-**an poss**tray?*
   Would you like dessert?

17. *feelaytess day bakkala-o*
cod in tomato and pepper sauce

1. *soap-a day feethayoss*
noodle soup

16. *pie-elya val-enthyanna*
rice and chicken, shellfish and vegetables

2. *kotheetho*
chicken, meat and vegetable stew

15. *lomo day mairlootha*
hake cutlet

3. *pol-yo al a-heelyo*
chicken with garlic

14. *tairnayra assatha*
roast veal

4. *tharthoo-ayla*
spicy fish and seafood stew

13. *kal-yoss madreelayn-ya*
tripe in spicy paprika and chorizo sausage sauce

5. *pattattass freetass*
chips

MENÚ

Starters – Sopas y entremeses
1. sopa de fideos
16. paella valenciana
Fish – Pescados y mariscos
4. zarzuela
17. filetes de bacalao
15. lomo de merluza
Meat – Carnes y aves
2. cocido
12. chuletas de cordero
14. ternera asada
3. pollo al ajillo
13. callos a la madrileña
Vegetables – Legumbres y verduras
10. ensalada mixta o rusa
11. judías verdes
5. patatas fritas
Desserts – Postres
6. queso
9. helados
7. flan
8. tarta helada

6. *kayso*
cheese

12. *choolaytass day kordayro*
lamb chops

7. *flan*
creme caramel

11. *hoothee-ass vairdess*
green beans

8. *tarta el-atha*
ice cream gateau

9. *el-athoss*
ice cream

10. *ensa-latha meexta*
(roossa)
mixed (Russian) salad

a la plancha
– grilled
a la romana
– fried in batter

Menú del día is the set menu for the day

You will find a wider choice of meat on p.25, vegetables on p.26 and fish on p.29

Ordering drinks

1. *Parra bebb**air**?*
   What would you like to drink?
3. *Day la kassa?*
   House wine?
5. Kon gas o seen gas?
   Fizzy or still?

2. *Oona bott-**el**ya day veeno teento (blanco/ross**atho**).*
   A bottle of red (white/rosé) wine.
4. *See, day la kassa, ee oon aggwa meenay-**ral**.*
   Yes, house wine, and some mineral water.

Paying and querying

un cuchillo
*oon koo**chill**-yo*
a knife

un tenedor
*oon tenay**thor***
a fork

una cuchara
*oona koo**charr**a*
a spoon

un vaso
oon vasso
a glass

1. *Mass pan, por fav**vor**.*
   Some more bread, please.
3. *Es-**sta** bee-**en**?*
   Do you like it?
5. *Oy-ga! La kwenta, por fav**vor**.*
   May I have the bill, please.

2. *Otra koo**charr**a, por fav**vor**.*
   Another spoon, please.
4. *See, mwee bee-**en**.*
   Yes, it's very nice.
6. *Eye oon err.-**or** a-key.*
   There is a mistake here.

21

Helados — *El-athoss* — Ice cream

fresa
fraysa
strawberry

nata
nahta
cream

piña
peenya
pineapple

pistacho
*pee**stacho***
pistachio

vainilla
*v-eye-**neel**ya*
vanilla

1. **Tyay**nen el-**athoss**?
   Have you any ice creams?

3. *Oono day choko**lah**-tay,
   por fav**vor**.*
   A chocolate one, please.

2. *See, day choko**lah**-tay,
   peenya ee fraysa.*
   Yes, chocolate, pineapple and
   strawberry.

4. **Gran**day o pekk**ayn**-yo?
   Large or small?

Self-service

Self-service restaurants offer a wide variety of meals. Some have a microwave to heat up your main course after you've eaten your starters.
Follow these instructions:

CALIENTE SU PLATO
Ponga el plato en el horno.
Apriete el botón.
Saque su plato cuando se apague la luz o suene la señal.
Para abrir la puerta introducir el dedo en el círculo y accionar hacia abajo.

Place plate inside oven.
Press button.
Your plate is ready when the light goes out or the buzzer sounds.
To open the door put your finger in the ring and move it downwards.

1. **Est**ay, por fav**vor**.
   Some of that, please.

2. *Kon vair**doo**rass?*
   With vegetables?

3. **Est**ass ee akk**ell**yass.
   These and those.

SHOPPING

abierto – open   *cerrado* – closed

Most shops are open from about 9.00 a.m. to 1.00 p.m. and again from 4.00 p.m. or 4.30 p.m. to 8.00 p.m.

ultramarinos
alimentación   all these sell food
comestibles

So do these: *supermercado* (supermarket) and
                                 hipermercado (hypermarket), and of course
                                 the *mercado* (market) itself where you will often
                                 get the best choice of fresh food.

HOW TO ASK

¿Tiene –? **(Tyay***nay* –?)   Have you any –?
Quisiera   un kilo de (manzanas)
*Keesee-***ay***ra*   *oon keelo day (man***thann***ass)*
I'd like   a kilo of (apples)

                                     medio kilo (cuarto kilo)
                                     mayth-*yo keelo (kwarto keelo)*
                                     half a kilo (a quarter kilo)

                                     un poco de (queso)
                                     *oon poko day (***kay***so)*
                                     a little (cheese)

                                     una lonja de (jamón)
                                     *oona ***lon***-ha day (ham-***on***)*
                                     a slice of (ham)

¿Vale? *(***Va***-lay?)*   Is that enough?

Un poco más/menos   A little more/less.
(Oon poko mass/**may**noss)

Vale *(***Va***-lay)*   That's fine

¿Algo más? *(***Al***-go mass?)*   Would you like anything else?

¿Cuánto es? *(Kwanto ess?)*   How much is it?

Uno de esos   One of those
(Oono day **ay***soss)*

IMPORTANT
Use the pattern of conversation shown in the bakery for all other kinds of shopping. Always remember:
Hola, buenos días (tardes). Good morning (afternoon),
when entering a shop, and Adiós – Goodbye – when leaving.

Panadería — *Panna-thereeya* — Baker

1. *Ola, **bway**noss **dee**-ass.*
   Good morning.

2. ***Bway**noss **dee**-ass. Kay dess-**ay**an?*
   Good morning. What would you like?

3. ***Tyay**nay pan? Oona barra mayth-**yann**a, por fav**vor**.*
   Have you any bread?
   A medium-sized loaf, please.

4. *A-**see**?*
   Like this?

1. *Ee kwattro **bol**yoss.*
   And four rolls.

2. *A-key **tyay**nay. Al-go mass?*
   There you are. Would you like anything else?

3. *No, ay-so ess totho. Kwanto ess?*
   No, that's all. How much is that?

4. *Sonn – pess**ay**tass.*
   That's – pesetas.

5. *Add-**yoss**, **bway**noss **dee**-ass.*
   Goodbye.

Cakes you'll find in the Pastelería. One cake is un pastel *(oon past-el),* two – or more! – are pasteles *(past-**ay**less).*
If you want some sweets, ask for caramelos *(karra-**may**loss).*

Carnicería — *Karneetherree-a* — Butcher

VACA
vakka
some Beef

CORDERO
*kor**dayro***
some Lamb

POLLO
***pol**-yo*
some Chicken

CERDO
thairdo
some Pork

UN PATO
oon patto
a Duck

TERNERA
*tair**nayra***
some Veal

ASADO
*ass-**atho***
Roast

CALLOS
***kal**-yoss*
some Tripe

CAZA
***ka**-tha*
some Game

RIÑONES
*reen**yonn**ess*
some Kidneys

HÍGADO
***ee**gatho*
some Liver

CARNE PICADA
*karnay pee**katha***
some Mince

CONEJO
*kon-**ay**ho*
some Rabbit

SOLOMILLO
*solo**meel**yo*
Fillet

CHULETAS
*choo**lay**tass*
Chops

COSTILLAS
*kost**eel**yass*
Ribs

Cold meat

JAMÓN SERRANO
*ham-**on** serranno*
some Cured Ham

JAMÓN DE YORK
*ham-**on** day York*
some Boiled Ham

UNA EMPANADA
*oona empan-**atha***
a Meat Pie

MORCILLA
*mor**theel**-ya*
Black Pudding

SALCHICHAS
*(Sal-**chee**chass)*
are different kinds
of Pork Sausages:

BUTIFARRA
*booty-**farra***

CHORIZO
*chor**ree**tho*
(hot and spicy)

LONGANIZA
*longa-**nee**tha*

SALCHICHÓN
*sal-chee**chon***
(salami-type)

SOBRASADA
*sobra-**satha***

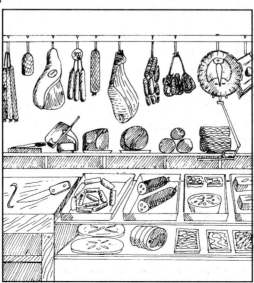

Verduras — *Vairdoorass* — Vegetables

in English order

ALCACHOFAS
al-kachofass
some Artichokes

ESPÁRRAGOS
esparragoss
some Asparagus

BERENJENAS
berren-haynass
some Aubergines

AGUACATES
aggwa-kattess
some Avocados

HABAS
abbass
some Broad Beans

JUDÍAS VERDES
hoothee-ass vairdess
some Green Beans

COL (COLES)/REPOLLO
kol (kol-ess)/ ray**pol**-yo
some Cabbage(s)

ZANAHORIAS
thannahory-ass
some Carrots

APIO
app-yo
some Celery

GARBANZOS
garbanthoss
some Chickpeas

MAÍZ
my-eeth
some Corn

un PEPINO
oon paypeeno
a Cucumber

AJO
a-ho
some Garlic

LENTEJAS
lentayhass
some Lentils

una LECHUGA
oona lechooga
a Lettuce

CHAMPIÑONES
champeen-yonness
some Mushrooms

Fruit & Vegetables

¿Tiene ...?
Tyaynay ...?
Have you any ...?

ACEITUNAS
a-thaytoonass
some Olives

CEBOLLAS
thaybolyass
some Onions

GUISANTES
gheesantess
some Peas

un PIMIENTO
oon peemee-ento
a Pepper

PATATAS
pattattass
some Potatoes

ESPINACAS
espee-nakkass
some Spinach

TOMATES
tom-attess
some Tomatoes

Frutas — *Frootass* — Fruit

ALMENDRAS
*al-**mendr**ass*
some Almonds

MANZANAS
*man**thann**ass*
some Apples

ALBARICOQUES
*al-ba-ree**kokk**ess*
some Apricots

HIGOS
***ee**-goss*
some Figs

un POMELO
*oon pom**maylo***
a Grapefruit

UVAS
***oo**vass*
some Grapes

NUECES
*n**way**thess*
some Nuts

NARANJAS
*na-**ran**-hass*
some Oranges

MELOCOTÓN(ES)
*mellokko-**ton**(ess)*
a Peach(es)

PERAS
***pay**rass*
some Pears

una PIÑA
*oona **peenya***
a Pineapple

CIRUELAS
*theeroo-**ay**lass*
some Plums

FRESAS
***fray**sass*
some Strawberries

una SANDÍA
*oona san-**dee**ya*
a Watermelon

rutas y verduras

...iera ...
*...see-**ay**ra ...*
...e ...

PLATANOS
***platt**a-noss*
some Bananas

CEREZAS
*thai**rray**thass*
some Cherries

un LIMÓN
*oon lee**mon***
a Lemon

un MELON
*oon may-**lon***
a Melon

una BOLSA
oona bolsa
a bag

Alimentación — Groceries

in *English* order

Quisiera …
*Keesee-ay*ra …
I'd like …

★

CERVEZA
*thair**vay**tha*
some Beer

GALLETAS
*gal-**yett**ass*
some Biscuits/Cookies

MANTEQUILLA
*mantay**keel**-ya*
some Butter

QUESO
***kay**so*
some Cheese

CAFÉ
*kaff**ay***
some Coffee

HUEVOS
***way**voss*
some Eggs

ZUMO DE FRUTA
thoomo day froota
some Fruit Juice

MIEL
*mee-**el***
some Honey

MERMELADA
*mairmay-**latha***
some Jam

MARGARINA
*margha-**ree**na*
some Margarine

LECHE
***lech**ay*
some Milk

ACEITE
*a-**thay**tay*
some Oil

ARROZ
*a-**roth***
some Rice

AZÚCAR
*a-**thoo**kar*
some Sugar

TÉ
tay
some Tea

PAPEL HIGIÉNICO
*pappel ee-hee-**ay**neeko*
some Toilet Paper

DETERGENTE
*daytair-**hen**tay*
some Soap Powder

AGUA
aggwa
some Water

VINO TINTO/BLANCO
veeno teento/blanco
Red/White Wine

YOGURT
*yoh-**goor***
some Yoghurt

mostaza	sal	pimienta
*mos**tatha***	*sal*	*peem-**yen**ta*
Mustard	Salt	Pepper

28

Pescadería — *Peska-theree-ya* — Fish shop

Spain has an excellent variety of fish. Here is a selection of them:

Pesskathoss Fish	*Ma-reeskoss* Seafood
ALMEJAS *al-mayhass* some Clams	LENGUADO *leng-watho* some Sole
ATÚN *a-toon* some Tuna	MEJILLONES *mayheel-yonness* some Mussels
BACALAO *bakkala-o* some Cod	MERLUZA *mairlootha* some Hake
CALAMARES *kal-ammaress* some Squid	PEZ ESPADA *peth espatha* some Swordfish

Pescados – Mariscos

GAMBAS *gambass* some Prawns	UNA LANGOSTA *oona langosta* a Lobster	UNA TRUCHA *oona troocha* a Trout	SALMONETES *sal-monnaytess* some Red Mullet

WEIGHTS & MEASURES

DRY WEIGHTS **LIQUID MEASURES**

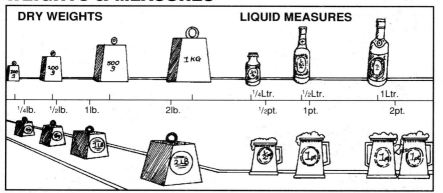

1 lb. = 454g.   1 kg. = 2 lb. 3 ozs. approx.   1 Ltr. = 1³/₄ pts. approx.

29

Droguería — Perfumería
Toiletries

ASPIRINAS
*aspee-**reen**ass*
some Aspirins

LOCIÓN ANTISÉPTICO
lothyon antisepteeko
some Antiseptic Lotion

CHAMPÚ
champoo
some Shampoo

ALGODÓN
*al-go**don***
some Cottonwool

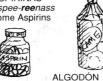

COMPRESAS/TAMPONES
*kom**pray**sass/
tam**pon**ess*
Sanitary Towels/Napkins
Tampons

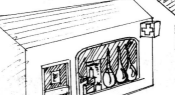

CONDONES
*kon-**don**ess*
some Condoms

PAÑUELOS DE PAPEL
*panyoo-**ay**loss day pap**pell***
Paper Handkerchiefs

UNA MÁQUINA DE AFEITAR
*oona **makk**-eena day affay-ee**tar***
a Razor

UNA VENDA
oona venda
a Bandage

PAÑALES
*pan**yal**-ess*
some Nappies

TIRITAS
*teer**ee**tass*
some Plasters/Band-aid

LOCIÓN CONTRA INSECTOS
lothyon contra eensektoss
some Insect Repellant

ACEITE BRONCEADOR
*a-**thay**tay bronthaya-**thor***
some Suntan Oil

ALIMENTOS INFANTILES
*allee**men**toss eenfan**teel**ess*
some Baby Food

UNAS GAFAS DE SOL
*oonass **gaff**ass day sol*
some Sunglasses

PASTA DE DIENTES
*pasta day dee-**en**tess*
some Toothpaste

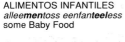

UN CEPILLO DE DIENTES
*oon thay**peel**yo day dee-**en**tess*
a Toothbrush

UN PEINE
*oon **pay**nay*
a Comb

UN DESODORANTE
*oon dessothor-**antay***
a Deodorant

JABÓN
*ha-**bon***
some Soap

WHO SELLS WHAT

Librería	Papelería	Quiosco
Bookshop	**Stationery**	**Newspapers**

un LIBRO
oon leebro
a Book

un PLANO (una mapa)
oon planno (oon mappa)
a Street Plan (Map)

un DICCIONARIO
oon deekth-yonarry-o
a Dictionary
(español-inglés)
(espanyol-eengless)
(Spanish-English)

una PELÍCULA
oona pel-ee-koola
a Film

un PERIÓDICO (inglés)
*oon payree-otheeko
(eengless)*
an (English)
Newspaper

un BOLÍGRAFO
oon bol-ee-graffo
a Pen

un LÁPIZ
oon lap-eeth
a Pencil

TABACOS

Estanco
Cigarettes, Postcards, Stamps

Ferretería
Hardware

POSTALES
posstal-ess
some Postcards

un SELLO
oon sellyo
a Stamp

un ABRELATAS
oon abbray-lattass
a Tin/Can Opener

un CAMPING-GAS
oon kamping gas
a Gas Bottle

CERILLAS
thayreelyass
Matches

una LINTERNA
oona leentairna
Torch/Flashlight

un ENCENDEDOR
oon enthenday-thor
a Lighter

una PILA
oona peela
a Battery

CIGARILLOS
theega-reelyoss
Cigarettes
(con filtro)
(with filter)

HILO
eelo
some Thread

un SACACORCHOS
oon sakka-korchoss
a Corkscrew

un DESTORNILLADOR
oon desstorneel-yathor
a Screwdriver

una AGUJA
oona aggoo-ha
a Needle

unas TIJERAS
oonass tee-hayrass
some Scissors

un ABRIDOR DE BOTELLAS
oon abry-thor day botellyass
a Bottle Opener

CUERDA
kwairda
some String/ Rope

una PLACA
oona plakka
an Ice Pack

FARMACIA – *Farmathya* – Chemist/Drugstore

Farmacias concentrate on medicine, baby needs and health foods. For toiletries, try a *Perfumería* or *Droguería* (see also Medical Section page 57 and Parts of the Body page 60)

¿Tiene algo para –?
***Tyay**nay algo parra –?*
Have you anything for –?

una garganta irritada
*oona gar**gan**ta eeree-**tatha***
a Sore Throat

la tos
la toss
a Cough

el dolor de estómago
*el do**lor** day es**stom**-aggo*
Stomach Ache

la fiebre del heno
*la fee-**ebb**ray del ayno*
Hay Fever

una picadura de insecto
*oona peeka**thoor**a day een**sek**to*
an Insect Bite

el dolor de oído
*el do**lor** day oy-**ee**tho*
Earache

las quemaduras de sol
*lass kayma**thoor**ass day sol*
Sunburn

el dolor de cabeza
*el do**lor** day ka**bay**tha*
Headache

la diarrea
*la dee-ar**ray**a*
Diarrhoea

el mareo
*el ma-**ray**o*
Seasickness

el estreñimiento
*el estrayn-yeem-**yen**to*
Constipation

Buying Clothes

1. Hola, buenos días. Quiero una camisa.
2. ¿Qué talla tiene?
3. La cuarenta. ¿Puede medirme?

1. *Ola bway**noss dee**-ass.*
   *Kee-**ay**ro oona ka-**mee**ssa.*
   Good morning, I'd like a shirt.

2. *Kay **tal**-ya **tyay**nay?*
   What size do you take?

3. La kwa-**ren**ta.
   Pwaythay may-**theer**may?
   I take size 40. Can you measure me?

32

1. **Pway**tho prob**bar**lo?
   May I try it on?

2. No see-**en**ta bee-**en**.
   It doesn't fit me.

3. Ess daymass-**yatho** pekk**ayn**-yo.
   It's too small.

4. Ess daymass-**yatho** gran**day**.
   It's too big.

5. Ess daymass-**yatho** karo.
   It's too dear.

Methods of Payment

1. May **goo**sta. May lo **lyay**vo.
   Kwanto kwesta?
   I like it. I'll take it.
   How much is it?

3. A-**thep**tan oo**stay**thess tar-**hay**tass
   day **kred**-eeto/ ay-ooro-**chekk**ess/
   dollaress **chekk**ess day **vya**-hay?
   Do you take credit cards/
   Eurocheques/travellers'
   cheques, dollars?

2. **Pass**ay por **ka**-ha.
   Please go to the cash desk.

4. **Grath**yass.
   Thank you.

5. Day natha.
   Not at all.

33

Clothes

un vestido
oon vesteetho
a dress

un traje de baño
oon tra-hay day banyo
a swimming costume

una camisa
oona ka-meessa
a shirt

una falda
oona falda
a skirt

un sombrero
oon sombrayro
a hat

unos pantalones
oonoss panta-lonness
some trousers

un jersey/suéter
oon hairsay/sweatair
a jumper

unas medias
oonass mayth-yass
some tights

unas sandalias
oonass sandal-yass
some sandals

unos calcetines
oonoss kalthay-teeness
some socks

un impermeable
oon eempairmay-abblay
a raincoat

un cinturón
oon theentoo-ron
a belt

unos guantes
oonoss gwantess
some gloves

un pañuelo
oon panyoo-aylo
a handkerchief

unos zapatos
oonoss tha-pattoss
some shoes

un pantalón corto
oon panta-lon korto
some shorts

CLOTHING SIZES — British and Continental

Clothing sizes are approximate — check your measurements!

WOMEN
Dresses/Suits

British	34	36	38	40	42	44
Continental	40	42	44	46	48	50

Stockings

British	8	8½	9	9½	10	10½
Continental	0	1	2	3	4	5

Shoes

British	4	5	6	7	8	9
Continental	37	38	39	41	42	43

MEN
Suits/Coats

British	36	38	40	42	44	46
Continental	46	48	50	52	54	56

Shoes

British	5	6	7	8	9	10	11
Contin'tal	38	39	41	42	43	44	45

Shirts

British	14	14½	15	15½	16	16½
Continental	36	37	38	39	41	42

BANKS

You can change money or traveller's cheques at banks like these ...

... but not always at one like this – it's a savings bank.

BANKING HOURS are roughly 9.00 a.m. to 2.00 p.m., Monday to Friday, 9.00 a.m. to 12.30 p.m. or 1.00 p.m. on Saturdays.

Public Holidays

New Year's Day	January 1	*Año Nuevo*
Epiphany	January 6	*Epifanía*
St. Joseph's Day	March 19	*San José*
Maundy Thursday		*Jueves Santo*
Good Friday		*Viernes Santo*
Easter Monday		*Lunes de Pascua*
Labour Day	May 1	*Día del Trabajo*
Corpus Christi	early June	*Corpus Christi*
St. James's Day	July 25	*Santiago Apóstol*
Assumption	August 15	*Asunción*
Columbus Day	October 12	*Hispanidad*
All Saints' Day	November 1	*Todos los Santos*
Immaculate Conception Day	December 8	*Inmaculada Concepción*
Christmas Day	December 25	*Navidad*

There is a swarm of local holidays.

Currency: Peseta

dinero/moneda
deenayro/monnaytha
money

un billete
oon beel-yaytay
a note

1. *Oy-ga, por favvor,*
   ***don**day eye oon banco?*
   Excuse me please, where is
   the nearest bank?

2. *Es-**sta** al-**yee**, en la **pla**-tha.*
   It's over there, in the square.

1. *Keesee-**ay**ra kamb-**yar** deenayro:*
   *ay-**oo**ro-**chekk**ess/ **lee**brass estair-*
   *leenass/ oon **chekk**ay day **vya**-hay.*
   I'd like to change some money:
   Eurocheques/pounds/
   a traveller's cheque/dollars.

3. *May feerma a-key.*
   Please sign here.

2. *Soo passa**por**tay, por favvor.*
   Your passport, please.

4. ***Pass**ay por **ka**-ha.*
   Please collect the money from
   the cashier.

Post Office — *Correos*

*Por favv**or**, **don**day es-**sta** korr**ay**oss?*
Where is the post office, please?

Buying Stamps — *Sellos*

Stamps can be bought at the tobacconist's *(Estanco)* – look for the sign *TABACOS* – and often at a *quiosco*. Since both are in the E.E.C., the postage rate for Britain is the same as within Spain. Tell them if you are sending postcards, since they are cheaper than letters.

Some larger post offices will change money and cash Eurocheques – look for *Cambio* signs.

1. *Oon sell-yo parra esta karta (pos**tal**), por favv**or**.*
   I'd like some stamps for this letter (postcard).

2. *Kwanto ess?*
   How much is it?

Telephone — *Teléfono*

¿Donde hay un telefono? ★

*Donday eye oon tell-**eff**ono?*
Where is there a phone?

Emergency: police, dial 091;
ambulance, fire brigade various numbers
(from 1992, dial 112 for all three.)

*Teléfono
Internacional*
Public
Telephone

¿Puedo llamar por telefono? ★

*Pwaytho lyam**mar** por tell-**eff**ono?*
May I use the phone?

To ring Britain, dial 07, wait for a second
tone, then dial 44 followed by the U.K.
code (leave off the first 0).

U.S. and Canada	dial 07 then	1
Australia	dial 07 then	61
New Zealand	dial 07 then	64
Eire	dial 07 then	353

Ringing Home

Look for phones marked *Teléfono internacional* — or the *Teléfonica office* (pay
afterwards). Phones are automatic, with full instructions in several languages.

Teléfonos

1. Quisiera llamar a Inglaterra.

★ 2. Quiero hacer una llamada a cobro revertido.

3. ¡Digame! ★

★ 4. ¿Podriá hablar con —?

1. *Keesee-**ay**ra lyam**mar** a Eengla-**terra**.*
   I'd like to ring England.

2. *Kee-**ay**ro ath-**air** oona lyam**matha** a kobbro rayvair-**tee**tho.*
   I'd like to make a reverse-charge (collect) call.

3. *Deega-may!*
   Hallo.

4. *Pod-**reeya** ab**lar** con …?*
   May I speak to — please?

Finding the way

¿Dónde está?
Donday es-sta?
Where is?

1. Oiga, por favor, ¿dónde está (la carretera de Blanes)?

2. Cruce la calle y coja la primera a la derecha.

3. ¿Puede indicármelo en el mapa?

4. ¿Está lejos?

1. *Oy-ga por favvor, donday es-sta (la karray-tayra day Blanness)?*
   Excuse me, where is (the road to Blanes)?

2. *Kroothay la kal-yay ee ko-ha la preemayra a la dayraycha.*
   Cross the road and take the first right.

3. *Pwaythay eendee-karmaylo en el mappa?*
   Could you show me on the map?

4. *Es-sta lay-hoss?*
   Is it far?

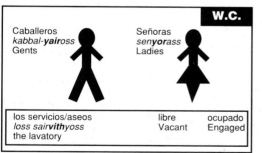

W.C.

Caballeros
kabbal-yaiross
Gents

Señoras
senyorass
Ladies

los servicios/aseos
loss sairvithyoss
the lavatory

libre
Vacant

ocupado
Engaged

todo recto
totho recto
straight on

a la izquierda
a la eethk-yairda
to the left

a la derecha
a la dayraycha
to the right

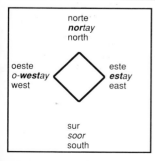

norte
nortay
north

oeste
o-westay
west

este
estay
east

sur
soor
south

antes/después
antess/despwess
before/after

en la esquina
en la eskeena
on the corner

el cruce
el kroothay
the crossroads

cerca de
thairka day
near to

enfrente de
enfrentay day
opposite

el semáforo
el semmafforo
traffic lights

Me he perdido
May ay pairdeetho
I'm lost

junto a/al lado de
hoonto a/al latho day
next to

La ciudad
La th-yoothath
The town

la Oficina de Turismo
*la offee-**thee**na day Too**rees**mo*
the Tourist Office

la comisaría
*la kommeesa-**ree**ya*
the police station

el Ayuntamiento
*el a-yoontam-**yen**to*
Town Hall

el castillo
*el ka**steel**yo*
the castle

el banco
el banco
the bank

el mercado
*el mair**katho***
the market

las tiendas
*lass tee-**en**dass*
the shops

la plaza
*la **pla**-tha*
the square

la catedral
*la kattay-**dral***
the cathedral

la iglesia
*la ee**glay**seeya*
the church

la estación
*la estath-**yon***
the station

la estación de autobuses
*la estath-**yon** day ow-to**boos**ess*
the bus station

la montaña
*la mon**tan**ya*
the mountain

el hotel
*el oh**tell***
the hotel

el museo
*el moo**ssay**o*
the museum

el río
èl ree-o
the river

el puente
*el **pwen**tay*
the bridge

Road Travel

What kind of road traveller are you?

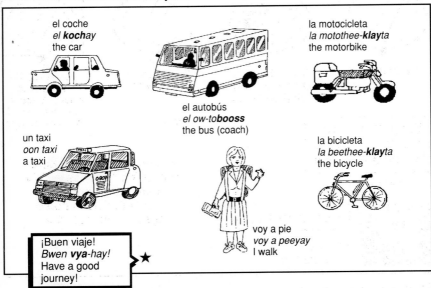

el coche
*el **koch**ay*
the car

el autobús
*el ow-to**booss***
the bus (coach)

la motocicleta
*la motothee-**klay**ta*
the motorbike

un taxi
oon taxi
a taxi

voy a pie
voy a peeyay
I walk

la bicicleta
*la beethee-**klay**ta*
the bicycle

¡Buen viaje!
*Bwen **vya**-hay!*
Have a good journey!

Round road signs tell you to do or not to do something. Square or oblong signs give information, and triangular signs warn you of danger.

CEDA EL PASO
300m
Give way

Crossroads with priority to the road on the <u>right</u>

Your right of way over side roads

Danger

Your right of way at crossroads

No longer your right of way

Variations on a No Parking theme

No parking

No parking on the right on even-numbered days

No parking on the right

(and vice versa)

ZONA AZUL parking disc needed *(disco de estacionamiento)*: from tobacconists

Dejen Paso Libre

Prohibido aparcar

No parking

Aparcarmiento

Parking permitted!

A sign including the word **"prohibido"** or **"prohibida'** means something is forbidden. Check these pages to find out what.

Motorway signs

Autopista = motorway

Motorway junction

To the motorway for Cádiz

Area servicio = service area
Salida means motorway exit. In Catalonia you will see **Sortida** instead.

Toll booth – get your money ready

Customs post

Start of town or village

End of town or village

Recommended **minimum** speed

U-turn possible ahead

1.

No entry

2.

DESVIACIÓN

Diversion

Prohibido de adelantar
No overtaking

Puesto de socorro
First Aid Post

PEATÓN/PEATONES
Pedestrians –
keep to the LEFT
on the open road

CRUCE PELIGROSO

Dangerous crossroads

CUIDADO

Caution

DESPACIO

Slow

PELIGRO

Danger

USO OBLIGATORIO CINTURÓN DE SEGURIDAD

Seatbelts compulsory.
You must always wear
a seatbelt when driving
in Spain.

Snow chains
obligatory

Fire danger:
Do **not** light
fires, matches,
cigarettes, etc.,
where you see
this sign

Car Hire — *Alquiler de coches*

1. **Bway**noss **dee**-ass, keesee-**ay**ra alkee**lar** oon **koch**ay.
   Good morning, I'd like to hire a car.

2. Kay **klass**ay day **koch**ay kee-**ay**ray? Pekk**ayn**-yo, **gran**day, mayth-**yanno**?
   What sort of car? Small, large, medium?

1. Parra oon dee-a? Parra oona se**mann**a?
   For one day? For one week?

2. Kwal ess la ta-**ree**fa?
   What is the rate?

3. Pwaytho day-**har** el **koch**ay en Ba**lenth**ya?
   May I leave the car in Valencia?

4. A-key **tyay**nay mee pair**mee**so day kondoo-**theer**.
   Here is my driving licence.

Buying Fuel — *Gasolinera/Estación Servicio*

Perdón, ¿hay una gasolinera cerca?

*Pair**don**, eye oona*
*gassolee-**nay**ra thairka?*
  Is there a gas/petrol station near
  here?

gasolina	aire
*gasso**lee**na*	**eye**-ray
petrol/gas	air
normal	sin plomo
*nor-**mal***	*seen plomo*
2-star	lead-free
súper	agua
***soo**pair*	*aggwa*
4-star	water
gasóleo	
*gas-**olla**yo*	
diesel	
aceite	
*a**thay**tay*	
oil	

motores dos tiempos
*mottoress doss tee-**emp**oss*
2-stroke mixture

Abierto Día y Noche — Open Day and Night

1. ¿Cuánta gasolina quiere?

2. ¿Normal o súper?

3. Lleno, por favor (de súper/ normal/sin plomo/gasóleo).

4. Por favor, compruebe el aceite.

5. ¿Cuánto es?

1. *Kwanta gasso**lee**na kee-**ay**ray?*
  How much gas/petrol would you
  like?

3. *L**lyay**no, por favv**or** (day **soo**pair/*
  *nor-**mal**/ seen plomo/gass-**olla**yo).*
  Fill it up, please (with super/
  normal/lead-free/diesel).

5. *Kwanto ess?*
  How much is that?

2. *Nor-**mal** o **soo**pair?*
  2-star or 4-star?

4. *Por favv**or**, komproo-**ay**bay el*
  *a**thay**tay.*
  Please check the oil.

Very few places accept credit cards. Make sure you have plenty of cash!

Breakdowns and Repairs

1. He tenido una avería. ¿Puedo usar el teléfono, por favor?

2. ¿Dónde está el garage más cercano?

1. *Ay teneetho oona avvair-reeya. Pwaytho oosar el tell-effono, por favvor?*
   I have broken down. May I use your phone, please?

2. *Donday es-sta el ga-rahay mass thairkanno?*
   Where is the nearest garage?

1. ¿Qué le pasa?

2. El *– no va bien.

3. ¿Cuánto tardarán?

4. ¿Cuánto le debo?

5. Muchas gracias.

1. *Kay lay passa?*
   What's the matter?

2. *El *– no va bee-en.*
   The *– isn't working.

3. *Kwanto tarda-ran?*
   How long will it take?

4. *Kwanto tarda-ran?*
   How much do I owe you?

5. *Moochass grathyass.*
   Thank you very much.

*For a selection of car components and things that might go wrong, see page 48.

On Two and Four Wheels

Necesito un –
*Naythay-**see**to oon –*
I need –

El motor se calienta.
*El mo**tor** say kal**yen**ta.*
The engine is overheating.

El – no funciona.
*El – no foonth-**yona**.*
The – isn't working.

El motor se para.
*El mo**tor** say parra.*
The engine is stalling.

Car, Bicycle and Motorcycle parts (in *English*) order

1. el filtro del aire
   *el **feel**tro del **eye**-ray*
   the Air Filter

2. la batería
   *la battay-**ree**ya*
   the Battery

3. los frenos
   *los **fray**noss*
   the Brakes

4. una bombilla
   *oona bom**bee**lya*
   a Bulb

5. el cable de freno (marchas)
   *el **kabb**lay day frayno (**mar**chass)*
   the Brake (Gear) Cable

6. el carburador
   *el karboora-**thor***
   the Carburettor

7. la cadena
   *la ka**day**na*
   the Chain

8. el aire
   *el **eye**-ray*
   the Choke

9. el embrague
   *el em**bragg**ay*
   the Clutch

10. el distribuidor
    *el deestreebwee-**thor***
    the Distributor

11. el sistema eléctrico
    *el see**stay**ma ay-**lek**treeko*
    the Electrical System

12. el motor
    *el mo**tor***
    the Engine

13. el tubo de escape
    *el toobo day es**kapp**ay*
    the Exhaust

14. la correa del ventilador
    *la kor**ray**a del venteela-**thor***
    the Fan Belt

15. el cuadro
    *el **kwa**dro*
    the Frame

16. la horquilla delantera
    *la or**keel**ya daylan**tay**ra*
    the Front Fork

17. un fusible
    *oon foo**see**blay*
    a Fuse

18. una junta
    *oona **hoon**ta*
    a Gasket

19. la caja de cambios
    *la **ka**-ha day **kamb**yoss*
    the Gearbox

20. las marchas
    *lass **mar**chass*
    the Gears

21. el manillar
    *el man**neel**-**yar***
    the Handlebars

22. los faros
    *los **far**ross*
    the Headlights

23. una cámara de aire
    *oona **kamm**ara day **eye**-ray*
    an Inner Tube

24. la llave de encendido
    *la **lyav**vay day enthen-**dee**tho*
    the Ignition Key

25. una perdida (de aceite)
    *oona pair**dee**tha (day a**thay**tay)*
    an (Oil) Leak

26. las luces
    *lass **loo**thess*
    the Lights

27. el portaequipajes
    el porta ekkeepa-hess
    the Luggage Carrier

28. una tira elastica
    *oona teera ay**las**teeka*
    a Luggage Elastic

29. un guardabarros
    *oon gwarda-**barr**oss*
    a Mudguard

30. una tuerca
    oona twairka
    a Nut

31. un bidón de gasolina
    *oon bee**thon** day gasso**lee**na*
    a Jerry Can

32. el juego de platinos
    *el hoo-**aygo** day plat**ee**noss*
    the Points

33. la bomba
    la bomba
    the Pump

34. el radiador
    *el rathya-**thor***
    the Radiator

35. la bolsa del sillín
    *la bolsa del seel**yeen***
    the Saddlebag

36. un tornillo
    *oon tor**nee**lyo*
    a Screw

37. un destornillador
    *oon destorneelya-**thor***
    a Screwdriver

38. un amortiguador
    *oon ammorteegwa-**thor***
    a Shock Absorber

39. el silenciador
    *el seelenthya-**thor***
    the Silencer

40. una llave inglesa
    oona l**yavv**ay een**gless**a
    a Spanner

41. una bujía
    *oona boo-**hee**ya*
    a Sparking Plug

42. los radios
    *loss **rath**yoss*
    the Spokes

43. un juego de herramientas
    *oon hoo-**aygo** day erram-**yen**tass*
    a Tool Kit

44. un neumático
    *oon nayoo-**matt**eeko*
    a Tyre

45. la presión de las ruedas
    *la press**yon** day lass roo-**ay**thass*
    the Tyre Pressure

46. una válvula
    *oona **val**voola*
    a Valve

47. una rueda
    *oona roo-**ay**tha*
    a Wheel

48. el parabrisas
    *el parra-**bree**sass*
    the Windscreen

cadenas para la nieve
*ka**day**nass parra la nee-**ay**vay*
Snow Chains

un pinchazo
*oon peen**chatho***
a puncture

un casco
oon kasko
a Crash Helmet

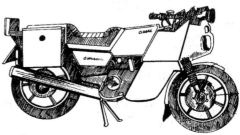

Rail Travel

Estación del Ferrocarril
Railway Station

¿Dónde está la estación?
Donday es-**sta** la estath-**yon**?
Where is the station?

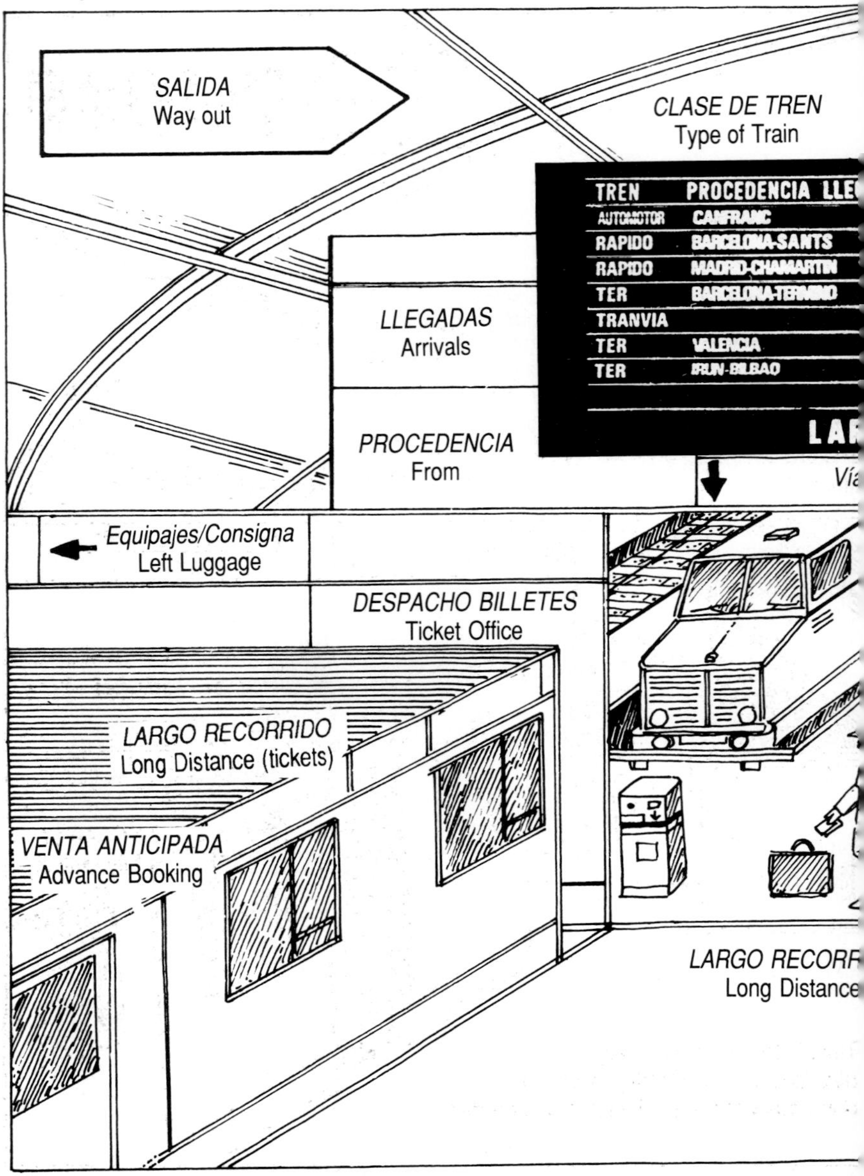

SALIDA
Way out

CLASE DE TREN
Type of Train

TREN	PROCEDENCIA	LLE
AUTOMOTOR	CANFRANC	
RAPIDO	BARCELONA-SANTS	
RAPIDO	MADRID-CHAMARTIN	
TER	BARCELONA-TERMINO	
TRANVIA		
TER	VALENCIA	
TER	IRUN-BILBAO	

LLEGADAS
Arrivals

PROCEDENCIA
From

LAR

Ví

Equipajes/Consigna
Left Luggage

DESPACHO BILLETES
Ticket Office

LARGO RECORRIDO
Long Distance (tickets)

VENTA ANTICIPADA
Advance Booking

LARGO RECORR
Long Distance

*The *Talgo* and the *Ter* are the fastest trains. You have to pay a supplement on them, and it's best to book in advance.

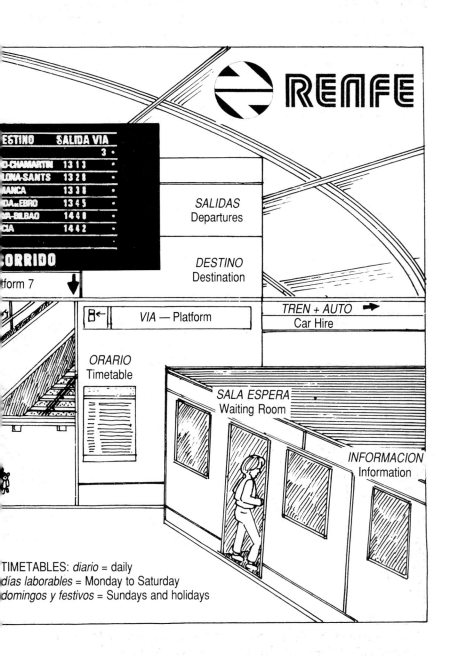

TIMETABLES: *diario* = daily
días laborables = Monday to Saturday
domingos y festivos = Sundays and holidays

Buying Tickets: Basic Pattern

2. ¿Ida o ida y vuelta?

1. Por favor, un billete de segunda clase para Madrid.

3. Ida solamente. ¿Cuánto es?

4. Quisiera reservar un asiento/ una litera/un coche cama.

¿Adónde va?
*Ad**don**day va?*
Where are you going?

Voy a –
Voy a –
I'm going to –

de primera clase
*day preemayra klassay
1st class

¿Fumador o no fumador?
*Fooma-**thor** o no fooma-**thor**?*
Smoker or non-smoker?

1. *Por favvor, oon beelyay-tay day segoonda klassay* parra Madreeth.*
   A second-class ticket for Madrid, please.

2. *Eetha o eetha ee vwelta?*
   Single or return?

3. *Eetha sola-mentay. Kwanto ess?*
   Single. How much is it?

4. *Keesee-ayra raysairvar oon assyento/oona leetayra/ oon kochay kamma.*
   I'd like to reserve a seat/ couchette/sleeper.

1. *Por favvor, kay an-den parra Malaga?*
   Which is the platform for Malaga?

2. *An-den tress.*
   Platform 3.

3. *A kay ora sallay el tren?*
   What time does the train go?

2. Andén tres.

1. Por favor, ¿qué andén para Málaga?

3. ¿A qué hora sale el tren?

No fumar/
Se prohibe fumar
= No smoking

*This phrase will do just as well for asking about a seat on a bus, plane or park bench – or in a restaurant, theatre, etc.

1. *Es-sta okkoopatho?*
Is this seat taken?

2. *Ess estay el tren parra Ka-deeth?*
Is this the train for Cádiz?

Metro

Underground railway/subway

Both Madrid and Barcelona have a *Metro.* The fare is the same wherever you go.

1. Oono, por favvor.
One, please.

1. *Parra Chammarteen,*
kay leenaya naythay-seeto?
Which line goes to Chamartín?

2. *Daybo kambyar?*
Do I have to change?

53

Bus Travel

1. *A kay ora **sall**ay el
   ow-to**booss** parra To**lay**tho?*
   When does the bus for Toledo go?

3. *Estay ow-to**booss** va a —?*
   Does this bus go to —?

2. *Day **don**day **sall**ay el
   ow-to**booss** parra el **Pra**tho?*
   Where does the bus for
   the Prado Museum go from?

aquí
a-key
here

allí
*al-**yee***
there

aquéllo
*a-**kell**yo*
that one
over there

1. *Ess la estath-**yon**?*
   Is this the station?

2. *Komo say **lyay**-ga
   al a-**ay**ro-**pwair**to?*
   How do I get to the airport?

54

Air Travel

En el aeropuerto
*En el a-**ayro**-p**wair**to*
At the airport

el avión
*el avv-**yon***
the aeroplane

el vuelo
el vwaylo
the flight

1. *A kay ora **sall**ay el **prox**eemo
   vwaylo parra **Lon**dress?*
   When is the next flight for
   London?

2. *A lass **nway**vay ee dee-**eth**.*
   At 9.10.

3. *A kay ora daybo a**thair**
   la faktoorath-**yon**?*
   What time should I check in?

4. *Kwal ess el **noo**mayro del vwaylo?*
   What is the flight number?

1. *Kee-**ay**ro kamb**yar**
   (annoo**lar**) me
   beel**yay**-tay
   parra **est**ay vwaylo.*
   I'd like to change
   (cancel) my
   reservation
   on this flight.

2. *See sen**yor**a.
   Parra kay vwaylo?*
   Yes madam.
   For which flight?

Boats

Barcos ➡
To the Boats ➡

En el puerto
En el pwairto
At the harbour

un barco
oon barko
a boat

Paseos por la bahía
Trips round the bay

Salidas cada 30 minutos
Departures every 30
minutes

1. ¿De dónde sale el próximo barco para Palma?
2. ¿A que hora?
¿Cuánto dura el viaje?

1. *Day **don**day **sall**ay el **prox**eemo barko parra **Pal**-ma?*
   Where does the next boat for Palma go from?

2. *A kay ora?*
   When?

3. *Kwanto doora el **vya**-hay?*
   How long does the crossing take?

el mar
el mar
the sea

una barca
oona barka
a rowing boat

el hidroavión
el eedro-avvyon
the hovercraft

el muelle
el mwayl-yay
the pier

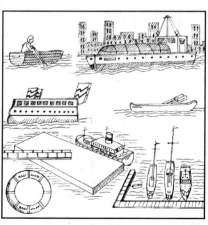

un salvavidas
oon salva-veethass
a lifebelt

el lago
el laggo
the lake

el bote salvavidas
el boatay salva-veethass
the lifeboat

el puerto deportivo
el pwairto dayporteevo
the yacht harbour

un barco de vela
oon barko day vayla
a yacht

56

Accidents and Illness

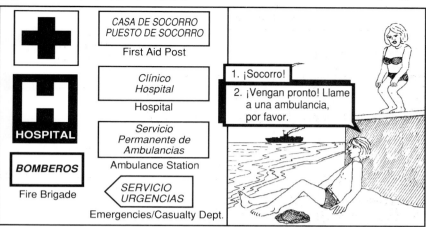

CASA DE SOCORRO PUESTO DE SOCORRO First Aid Post	1. ¡Socorro!
Clínico Hospital Hospital	2. ¡Vengan pronto! Llame a una ambulancia, por favor.
Servicio Permanente de Ambulancias Ambulance Station	
SERVICIO URGENCIAS Emergencies/Casualty Dept.	

HOSPITAL

BOMBEROS
Fire Brigade

1. *Sok**korro**!*
   Help!

2. ***Veng**an pronto! **Lyam**may a oona
   amboo-**lanth**ya, por fav**vor**.*
   Come quickly! Please call an
   ambulance.

Minor ailments: See *Farmacia* section page 32.

Calling the doctor/Making an appointment

a. Estoy enfermo/a.
   Necesito un médico.

b. Quisiera ver al
   médico. ¿Cuándo
   puede ser?

In case of accident, stop
the next passing car. The
driver is *obliged* to
take you to the nearest
First Aid centre.

> **Dr. Javier Losada**
> **Médico**

> **Medicina General**

Both these signs
are for doctors

> **CONSULTA:**
> **mañana 10 a 1 tarde 4 a 8**

Surgery Hours:
10 a.m.-1 p.m. 4 p.m.-8 p.m.

a. *E**stoy** en**fair**m/a*. Naythay**see**to
   oon **may**theeko.*
   I'm ill. I need a doctor.
   * see p. 72

b. *Keesee-**ay**ra vair al **may**theeko.
   Kwando **pway**thay sair?*
   I'd like to see the doctor. When
   can I come?

First Aid posts are free, but if you go to a doctor you will have to pay on the spot.

At the Doctor's (Parts of the body p.60)

1. **Don**day lay **dway**lay? Lay **dway**lay?
   Where does it hurt? Does that hurt?

2. May **dway**lay a-key. Tengo fee-**ay**bray (Tengo free-o). Ay vommee**tatho**.
   It hurts here. I have a temperature (I am cold). I have been sick.

3. Es-**sta** vakkoo**natho** kontra el **tett**anno?
   Have you been vaccinated against tetanus?

4. Kwanto tyempo lyayva en**fair**mo/a?*
   How long have you been ill?

5. **Estoy** to**mando estoss** meddeeka-**men**toss.
   I take these medicines.

*See p.72.

1. **Pway**thay **dar**may oona ray**thay**ta?
   Could you give me a prescription?

2. No **day**bay komair … (beb**bair** …).
   You must not eat … (drink).

3. (For a child):
   Kwantoss an**yoss tyay**nay?
   How old is he/she?

4. **Tyay**nay – an**yoss**.
   He/she's – years old.

5. Kay lay daybo?
   How much do I owe you?

When to take your medicine:	Things the doctor needs to know:
… veces al día (… times a day)	*(Soy …)* Soy … I'm …
cada … horas (every … hours)	alérgico/a* *allairheeko/a* allergic
antes/después de cada comida (before/after meals)	asmático/a *assmatteeko/a* asthmatic
para … días (for … days)	diabético/a epiléptico/a *dee-abetteeko/a aypee-lepteeko/a* diabetic epileptic
por las mañanas (in the mornings)	estoy embarazada *estoy embarra-thatha* I'm pregnant
por la noche (at night)	tengo la tensión alta *tengo la tensyon alta* I've high blood pressure
98·6°F = 37°C *alérgico etc. for men alérgica etc. for women	sufro algo del corazón ***soo**fro algo del korra**thon*** I've a heart condition

At the Dentist

Médico Dentista
Clínico Dental
Consulta
de 1 tarde

Surgery from 1 p.m.

1. Me duelen las muelas.

2. Quisiera solicitar una cita con el dentista.

3. ¿Le duele?

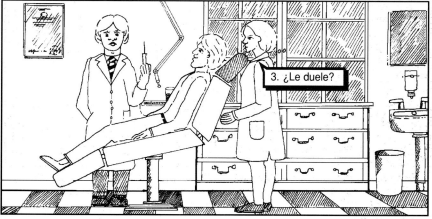

1. *May **dway**len lass **mway**lass.*
   I have toothache.

3. *Lay **dway**lay?*
   Does that hurt?

2. *Keesee-**ayra** soleetheetar oona theeta kon el den**tee**sta.*
   May I make an appointment to see the dentist?

Parts of the Body — listed alphabetically

el cuerpo
el kwairpo
The Body

Me duele aquí.
*May **dway**lay a-key.*
It hurts here.

el tobillo
*el to**bee**lyo*
the Ankle

el brazo
el bratho
the Arm

la espalda
*la es**pal**da*
the Back

el pecho
el paycho
the Chest

las orejas
*lass or**ray**-hass*
the Ears

el codo
el kodo
the Elbow

el ojo
*el **o**-ho*
the Eye

la cara
la karra
the Face

el dedo
el daytho
the Finger

el pie
el peeyay
the Foot

el pelo
el paylo
the Hair

la mano
la manno
the Hand

la cabeza
*la ka**bay**tha*
the Head

el corazón
*el korra**thon***
the Heart

la cadera
*la ka**day**ra*
the Hip

la rodilla
*la ro**deel**ya*
the Knee

la pierna
*la pee-**air**na*
the Leg

la boca
la bokka
the Mouth

el cuello
el kwellyo
the Neck

la nariz
*la na-**reeth***
the Nose

el hombro
el ombro
the Shoulder

el estómago
*el es**tom**-aggo*
the Stomach

los dientes
*loss dee-**en**tess*
the Teeth

la garganta
*la gar**gan**ta*
the Throat

el dedo del pie
el daytho del peeyay
the Toe

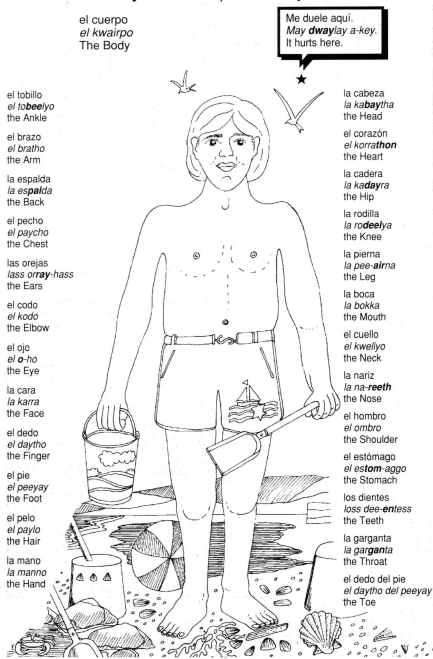

60

Sightseeing

Donday es-**sta** la
offee**thee**na day
Too**rees**mo?
   Where is the Tourist
   Office?

1. *Kay eye day eentay**ress**
   *en Barthel**lona**?*
   What is there to see in
   Barcelona?

2. *Eye el monna**stay**ree-o,*
   *el kasko **vyay**-ho …*
   There is the monastery, the
   old town …

3. *Kwando say **pway**thay*
   *veesee**tar** el monna**stay**ree-o?*
   When is the monastery open?

4. *Say **pway**thay veesee**tar** tot**hoss***
   *loss **dee**-ass es**thep**to loss **loo**ness.*
   It is open every day except
   Monday.

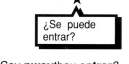

*Say **pway**thay en**trar**?*
May we go in?

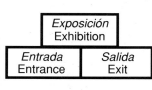

1. ***Tyay**nay oon planno*
   *day Santan**dair**?*
   Have you a town plan of
   Santander?

2. *Eye oon **ghee**-ya kay **abb**lay*
   *eeng**less**?*
   Is there an English-speaking
   guide?

Sports

1. **Don**day es-**tan** lass **pee**stass day **tay**neess?
   Where are the tennis courts?

2. Kwanto kwesta por dee-a / hoo-**ay**go/ora?
   How much is it per day/game/hour?

3. **Don**day es-**sta** el kampo day golf (la ply-a / la pees**thee**na)?
   Where is the golf course? (the beach/swimming pool).

4. **Don**day say **pway**thay prakteekar la peska?
   Where can you go fishing?

Skiing

1. Say **pway**thay to**mar** lekth-y**on**ess day es**kee**?
   Can I have some skiing lessons?

2. Klarro!
   Yes, of course.

3. May goosta-**ree**ya ay**kee**po day es**kee**.
   I'd like some skiing equipment.

Entertainments

1. ¿Hay algún partido de fútbol (alguna corrida) esta semana?
2. Quisiera dos localidades para esta noche (viernes por la tarde/noche).
3. ¿Sol o sombra?
4. ¿A qué hora empieza?

1. *Eye algoon parteetho day footboll (algoona korreetha) esta semanna?*
   Is there a football match (bullfight) on anywhere this week?

2. *Keesee-ayra doss lokallee-thathess para esta nochay (vee-airness por la tarday/nochay).*
   I'd like two tickets for this evening (Friday afternoon/evening)

3. *Soll o sombra?*
   On the sunny side or in the shade?

4. *A kay ora emp-yaytha?*
   When does it start?

Una corrida

Oona korreetha
A bullfight

On the piste

1. No sé esquiar.
2. Sé esquiar bien.

la pista
la peesta
the ski run

el telesquí
el tayleskee
the ski lift

esquí de fondo/ nórdico
eskee day fondo/ nordeeko
cross-country skiing

1. *No say eskeeyar.*
   I don't know how to ski.

2. *Say eskeeyar bee-en.*
   I'm good at skiing.

63

Making friends

1. **O-la. Ath**ay oon dee-a esstoo**pendo**, vair**dath?** Komo es-**sta** oo**steth?**
   Hello. What a lovely day, isn't it? How are you?

2. Mwee bee-**en** — ee oo**steth?**
   Fine thanks – and you?

3. May **lya**mmo —.
   Komo say **lyamma** oo**steth?**
   My name is –.
   What is your name?

4. **Est**ay ess me ma**rree**tho (me moo-**hair**), me **ee**-ho ee me **ee**-ha.
   This is my husband (my wife), my son and my daughter.

5. Moocho goosto.
   Pleased to meet you.

1. Esta ess me air**manna** (air**manno**).
   This is my sister (brother).

2. **Tyay**ness air**mann**oss ee air**mann**ass?
   Have you any brothers and sisters?

3. **Kwan**toss **any**oss **tyay**ness?
   How old are you?

4. Tengo **tray**thay **any**oss.
   I am 13.

Making conversation

1. Sus hijos son muy simpáticos. ¿De dónde es usted?
3. ¿Es la primera vez que viene en España?
4. ¿Le gusta aquí?
2. Soy de Londres.
5. Mucho.

1. *Sooss **ee**-hoss sonn mwee seem-**patt**eekoss? Day **don**day ess oo**steth**?*
   Your children are very nice. Where do you come from?

3. *Ess la pree**may**ra veth kay **vyay**nay en Es**pan**ya?*
   Is this your first visit to Spain?

5. *Moocho.*
   Very much.

2. *Soy day **Lon**dress.*
   I come from London.

4. *Lay goosta a-key?*
   Do you like it here?

Accepting an invitation

1. ¿Estás libre esta tarde?
2. ¿Te gustaría venir a vernos?
3. Estupendo. Me encantaría.
4. ¿A que hora nos encontramos?

Only London (*Londress*/Londres), Edinburgh (*Aydim**boor**go*/Edimburgo) and New York *(Noo-**ay**va York*/Nueva York) are translated into Spanish. Most other places in the British Isles and the rest of the English-speaking world have their names unchanged by the Spanish (more or less ...).

1. *Es**tass lee**bray esta **tar**day?*
   Are you free this evening?

3. *Estoo**pen**do. May enkanta-**ree**ya.*
   Wonderful. I'd love to.

2. *Tay goosta-**ree**ya ven**neer** a **vair**noss?*
   Would you like to come and see us?

4. *A kay ora noss encon**tramm**oss?*
   When shall we meet?

Visiting

1. *O-la, kay tal?*
   Hello, how are you?

2. *Bee-en.*
   Fine.

3. *See-entaytay. Seerva-tay.*
   Please sit down. Help yourself.

4. *Tay goosta lay-air/loss dayportess/ buy-lar/la moosseeka?*
   Do you like reading/sport/ dancing/music?

5. *May goosta …*
   I like …

6. *Sabbay mwee bwayno.*
   It tastes very good.

Saying goodbye

1. *Moochass grathyass por la vaylatha. A seetho estoopendo.*
   Thank you for this evening. It was wonderful.

2. *Day natha. Asta loo-aygo.*
   Not at all. Be seeing you.

Pests

If you don't fancy the local Casanova, one of these *might* work. If it doesn't, you could try half a brick hidden in your handbag ...

1. **Day**-haymay en path!
   Leave me alone!

2. **V-eye**-assay!
   Go away!

3. **Larg**attay!
   Push off!

Theft and Lost Property

1. May ann rob**batho** —.
   My – has been stolen.

2. Ay pairdeetho —.
   I have lost –.

mi bolso
me bolso
my bag

mi pasaporte
*me passa**por**tay*
my passport

mi dinero
*me dee**nay**ro*
my money

mi cámera
me camera
my camera

mis llaves
*meess **lyav**vess*
my keys

mis cheques de viaje
*meess **check**ess day **vya**-hay*
my traveller's cheques

nombre	dirección	¿cuándo?	¿dónde?
nombray	deerekth-**yon**	kwando	**don**day
name	address	when	where

Friends and Relations

Mi Familia
Me Fameelya
My Family

mi abuelo
*me **abway**lo*
my grandfather

mi abuela
*me **abway**la*
my grandmother

mi padre
*me **padd**ray*
my father

mi madre
*me **madd**ray*
my mother

un/mi amigo
*oon/me a**mee**go*
a/my friend (m)

mi hijo
*me **ee**-ho*
my son

mi hija
*me **ee**-ha*
my daughter

una/mi amiga
*oona/me a**mee**ga*
a/my friend (f)

el niño
el neenyo
the boy

la nina
la neenya
the girl

Countries and Nationalities

¿De dónde es usted?	Soy/Soy de …	Soy español	Soy española
*Day **don**day ess oo**steth**?*	*Soy/Soy day …*	*Soy espan**yol***	*Soy espan**yolla***
Where do you come from?	I am/I come from …	I'm Spanish [man]	I'm Spanish [woman]

Inglaterra	inglés/inglesa	Irlanda	irlandés/irlandesa
*Eengla**terra***	*een**gless**/een**gless**a*	*Eer**land**a*	*eerlan**dess**/**dess**a*
England	English	Ireland	Irish

Escocia	escocés/escocesa	Gales	galés/galesa
*Es**koth**ya*	*es**koth**ess/**thess**a*	***Ga**-less*	*ga-**less**/**less**a*
Scotland	a Scot	Wales	Welsh

los Estados Unidos	(norte) americano/a
*loss E**stath**oss Oo**nee**thoss*	*(**nor**tay) amayree**kanno**/a*
U.S.A.	(North) American

Australia	australiano/australiana
*Ow-**stral**ya*	*ow-stral**yanno**/a*
Australia	Australian

del Canadá	canadiense
*del Kanna-**da***	*kannad-**yen**say*
Canada	Canadian

Nueva Zelandia	nueva zelandés/desa
*Noo-**ay**va Thay**land**ya*	*noo-**ay**va thaylan**dess**/a*
New Zealand	a New Zealander

Around the Clock and Greetings

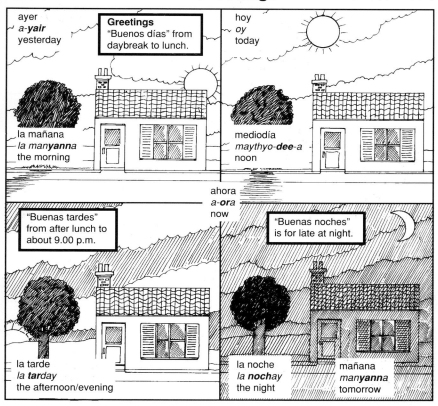

ayer
*a-**yair***
yesterday

Greetings
"Buenos días" from daybreak to lunch.

la mañana
*la man**yanna***
the morning

hoy
~ *oy*
today

mediodía
*maythyo-**dee**-a*
noon

ahora
*a-**ora***
now

"Buenas tardes" from after lunch to about 9.00 p.m.

"Buenas noches" is for late at night.

la tarde
*la **tar**day*
the afternoon/evening

la noche
*la **noch**ay*
the night

mañana
*man**yanna***
tomorrow

Days of the Week — la semana *(la semanna)*

lunes
***loo**ness*
Monday

martes
***mar**tess*
Tuesday

miércoles
*me-**airk**olless*
Wednesday

jueves
*hoo-**evv**ess*
Thursday

viernes
*vee-**air**ness*
Friday

sábado
***sabb**atho*
Saturday

domingo
*do**meeng**o*
Sunday

·69·

Seasons, months and weather

en la primavera — *en la preema-**vay**ra* — in spring

marzo
martho
<u>March</u>

mayo
m-eye-o
<u>May</u>

hace viento
***ath**ay vee-**en**to*
it's windy

pascua
paskwa
Easter

abril
*ab**reel***
<u>April</u>

llueve
*lyoo-**evv**ay*
it's raining

en el verano — *en el vay**rann**o* — in summer

junio
***hoo**nee-o*
<u>June</u>

agosto
*a-**gos**to*
<u>August</u>

hace sol
***ath**ay soll*
the sun shines

julio
***hoo**lee-o*
<u>July</u>

hace calor
ath**ay ka-**lor
it's hot

en el otoño — *en el ot**ton**yo* — in autumn

septiembre
*sept-**yem**bray*
<u>September</u>

noviembre
*nov-**yem**bray*
<u>November</u>

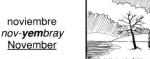

vendimia
*ven**deem**-ya*
wine harvest

octubre
*ok**too**bray*
<u>October</u>

hace frío
***ath**ay free-o*
it's cold

en el invierno — *en el eenv-**yair**no* — in winter

diciembre
*deeth-**yem**bray*
<u>December</u>

febrero
*feb**rair**o*
<u>February</u>

Navidad
*navvee-**thath***
Christmas

enero
*en-**air**o*
<u>January</u>

nieva
*nee-**ay**va*
it's snowing

Time

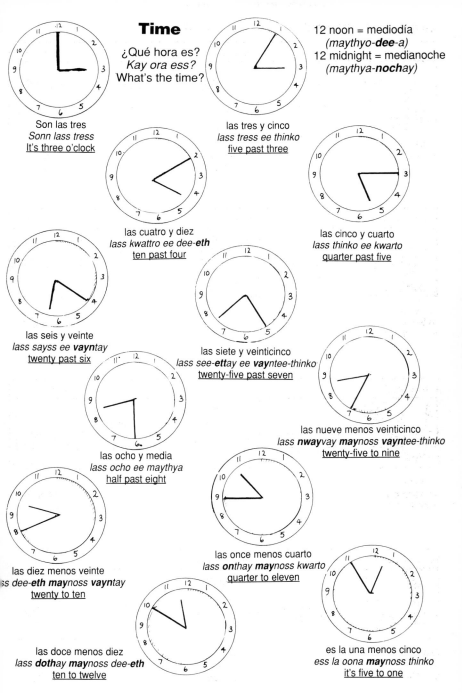

¿Qué hora es?
Kay ora ess?
What's the time?

12 noon = mediodía
*(maythyo-**dee**-a)*
12 midnight = medianoche
*(maythya-**noch**ay)*

Son las tres
Sonn lass tress
It's three o'clock

las tres y cinco
lass tress ee thinko
five past three

las cuatro y diez
*lass kwattro ee dee-**eth***
ten past four

las cinco y cuarto
lass thinko ee kwarto
quarter past five

las seis y veinte
*lass sayss ee **vayn**tay*
twenty past six

las siete y veinticinco
*lass see-**ett**ay ee **vayn**tee-thinko*
twenty-five past seven

las ocho y media
lass ocho ee maythya
half past eight

las nueve menos veinticinco
*lass **nway**vay **may**noss **vayn**tee-thinko*
twenty-five to nine

las diez menos veinte
*ss dee-**eth may**noss **vayn**tay*
twenty to ten

las once menos cuarto
*lass **on**thay **may**noss kwarto*
quarter to eleven

las doce menos diez
*lass **doth**ay **may**noss dee-**eth***
ten to twelve

es la una menos cinco
*ess la oona **may**noss thinko*
it's five to one

71

Shorthand Grammar
or How Spanish Works

Things: Nouns. In Spanish all nouns are thought of as either masculine (m.) or feminine (f.).

When talking about one thing only, i.e. **singular** (s.), **A** is *un* (m.) or *una* (f.), e.g. *un piso* a flat or floor, *una casa* a house.

If there is more than one, i.e. **plural** (pl.), add an *s*, e.g. *pisos* flats, *casas* houses.

The (singular) is *el* (m.):   *el piso* the flat, apartment.
                    la (f.):   *la casa* the house.

If the noun is plural, use *los* if it's masculine and *las* if it's feminine, e.g. *los pisos* the flats, *las casas* the houses.

Describing things: Adjectives. If a noun is masculine the adjective describing it will be too. If the noun is feminine or if there is more than one, the ending will change accordingly.

e.g. *un chico pequeño*   a small boy (m. sing.)
     una chica pequeña   a small girl (f. sing.)
     dos chicos pequeños   two small boys (m. pl.)
     dos chicas pequeñas   two small girls (f. pl.)

These adjectives have the same ending as the words they are describing. Some adjectives simply add *s* or *es*.

e.g. *una cerveza grande*   a large beer
     un libro inglés   an English book
     dos cervezas grandes   two large beers
     dos libros ingleses   two English books

This is *este* with masculine nouns, *esta* with feminine ones, and *esto* if you are not talking about a specific thing.
e.g. *¿Qué es esto?*   What's this?

It's mine: Possessives. The word for *my, your,* etc. depends on whether the **following** word is masculine, feminine or plural,

e.g. *mi piso* my flat, *mis libros* my books.

	s.	pl.		s.	pl.
my	*mi*	*mis*	our	*nuestro(a)*	*nuestros(as)*
your (s.)	*tu*	*tus*	your (pl.)	*vuestro(a)*	*vuestros(as)*
his, her, its	*su*	*sus*	their	*su*	*su*

There is no difference between his, her or its,
e.g.   *su hijo: his* or *her* son, *su casa: his* or *her* house.

People or things: Pronouns

"I", "you" *(yo, tú)* etc. are rarely used except for emphasis, since the ending of the verb shows quite clearly who you are talking about. Although *tú* is increasingly common, it is wise to use *usted* (plural *ustedes* and often shortened to *Vd./Vds.),* except with children and close friends. N.B. *Usted* uses the same ending of the verb as "he", "she" and "it".

Doing things: Verbs

Spanish has two verbs "to be". *Ser* is used to describe normal states, such as "They are Spanish", and for telling the time. *Estar* describes temporary states and where things are, e.g. "It is over there".

to be		ser	to be	estar
I am	(yo)	soy	I am	estoy
you are	(tú)	eres	you are	estás
he/she/it is	(él/ella)	es	he/she/it is	está
you are (polite s. form)	(usted)	es	you are (polite s. form)	está
we are	(nosotros)	somos	we are	estamos
you are (pl.)	(vosotros)	sois	you are (pl.)	estáis
they are	(ellos/ellas)	son	they are	están
you are (polite pl. (form)	(ustedes)	son	you are (polite pl. form)	están

to have	tener	to want	querer
I have	tengo	I want	quiero
you have	tienes	you want	quieres
he/she/it/Vd. has	tiene	he/she/it/Vd. wants	quiere
we have	tenemos	we want	queremos
you have (pl.)	tenéis	you want (pl.)	queréis
they/Vds. have	tienen	they/Vds. want	quieren

to be able	poder	to go	ir
I can	puedo	I go	voy
you can	puedes	you go	vas
he/she/it/Vd. can	puede	he/she/it/Vd. goes	va
we can	podemos	we go	vamos
you can (pl.)	podéis	you go (pl.)	vais
they/Vds. can	pueden	they/Vds. go	van

Saying no. Just put *no* before the verb,
e.g. *No hablo español* I don't speak Spanish.

Questions. The simplest and most usual way is just to speak a sentence as if it were a question,

e.g. *Hablo inglés.* I speak English.
¿Habla inglés? Do you speak English?

Booking Accommodation

Estimado Señor,   Dear Sir,

Hotels: Quisiera reservar una/dos habitación(*es) individual(*es)/doble(*s) (con baño/ducha) para — noches desde — hasta —.
I should like to book one/two single/double room(s) (with bath/shower) for — nights from — to —.

¿Qué cantidad requieran como depósito para la reserva de la(*s) habitación(*es)?
How much deposit do you require to book the room(s)?

Camping: Quisiera reservar una plaza (con electricidad) en su camping, a la sombra si es posible. Desearíamos estar — noches desde — hasta —.
I should like to book a pitch (with electricity) on your campsite, in the shade if possible. We wish to stay — nights from — to —.

Tenemos un coche/caravana/coche-cama y una tienda de campaña grande/pequeña (con toldo).
We have a car/caravan/motor caravan and a large/small tent (with awning).

¿Qué cantidad requieran como depósito para la reserva de la plaza?
How much deposit do you require to reserve the pitch?

Nuestro grupo/familia consistirá de — adultos y — niños(*s) de edades —.
Our group/family will consist of — adults and — child(ren) aged —.

Por favor haganos saber sus tarifas.
Please let us know your rates.

Muy atentamente,
Yours faithfully,

*add s or es if more than one.

Index

Comb

Here

Hobbies

Omelette

Once more

Sport

Square

Zarzuela

Numbers

0 *thayro*
cero

1 *oono*
uno

2 *doss*
dos

3 *tress*
tres

4 *kwattro*
cuatro

5 *thinko*
cinco

6 *sayss*
seis

7 *see-ettay*
siete

8 *ocho*
ocho

9 ***nway**vay*
nueve

10 *dee-**eth***
diez

11 ***on**thay*
once

12 ***doth**ay*
doce

13 ***treth**ay*
trece

14 *katt**orth**ay*
catorce

15 ***keen**thay*
quince

16 *dee-ethy-**sayss***
dieciséis

17 *dee-ethy-see-**ett**ay*
diecisiete

18 *dee-ethy-**och**o*
dieciocho

19 *dee-ethy-**nway**vay*
diecinueve

20 ***vayn**tay*
veinte

21 *vayntee-**oon**o*
veintiuno

22 *vayntee**doss***
veintidós

23 *vayntee**tress***
veintitrés

24 *vayntee**kwatt**ro*
veinticuatro

25 *vayntee**think**o*
veinticinco

26 *vayntees**sayss***
veintiséis

27 *vayntee see-**ett**ay*
veintisiete

28 *vayntee-**och**o*
veintiocho

29 *vayntee-**nway**vay*
veintinueve

30 *tray**een**ta*
treinta

31 *tray**een**ta ee oono*
treinta y uno

32 *tray**een**ta ee doss*
treinta y dos

33 *tray**een**ta ee tress*
treinta y tres

40 *kwarr**en**ta*
cuarenta

50 *think**wen**ta*
cincuenta

60 *sess**en**ta*
sesenta

70 *say**ten**ta*
setenta

80 *och**en**ta*
ochenta

90 *nov**en**ta*
noventa

100 *thee-**en***
cien

101 *thee-**en**to oono*
ciento uno

200 *doss thee-**en**toss*
doscientos

500 *keen-**yen**toss*
quinientos

1000 *meel*
mil

1200 *meel doss thee-**en**toss*
mil doscientos

2000 *doss meel*
dos mil

1st *pree**may**ro*
primero

2nd *seg**oon**do*
segundo

3rd *tair**thay**ro*
tercero